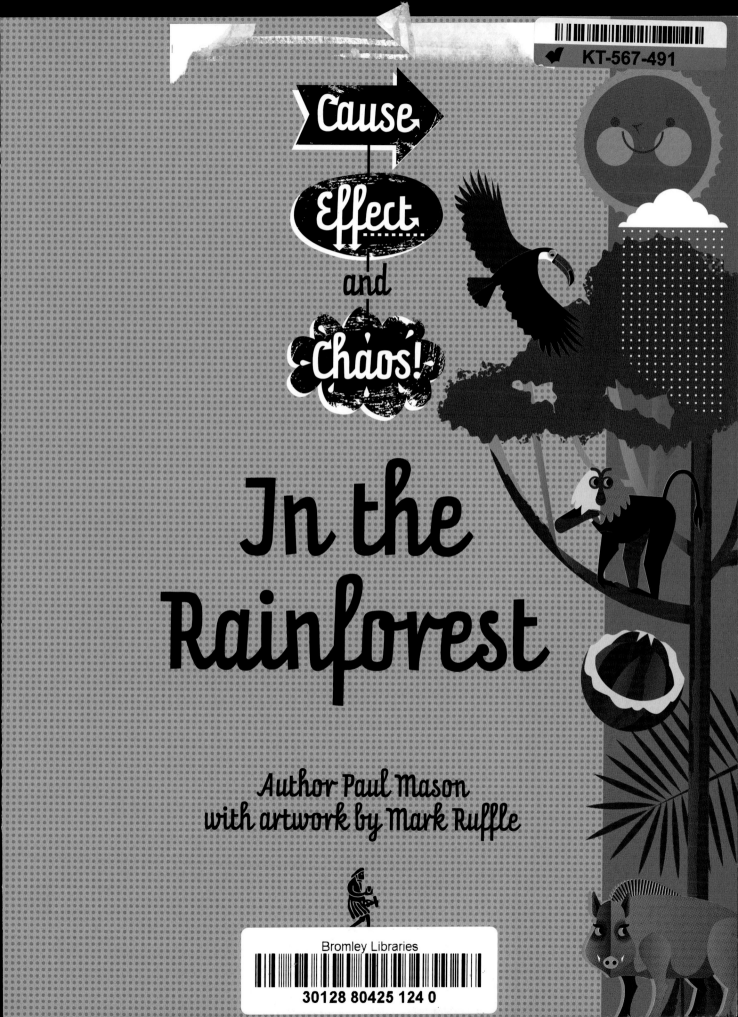

# Cause Effect and Chaos!

# In the Rainforest

Author Paul Mason
with artwork by Mark Ruffle

Published in paperback in Great Britain in 2020
by Wayland
Copyright © Hodder and Stoughton, 2018

Series editor: Paul Rockett
Series design and illustration: Mark Ruffle
www.rufflebrothers.com

ISBN 978 1 5263 0581 7

Printed in China

Wayland, an imprint of
Hachette Children's Group
Part of Hodder and Stoughton
Carmelite House
50 Victoria Embankment
London EC4Y 0DZ

An Hachette UK Company
www.hachette.co.uk

FSC
www.fsc.org

MIX
Paper from
responsible sources
FSC® C104740

# Contents

# Cause and Effect

Why do events happen? Usually it's because of something else that happened before.

You'll definitely be able to come up with examples of this from your own life. Just imagine:

You beg and plead with your parents for a new skateboard.

Weeks of pressure finally have an effect:

## a new skateboard!

Of course, the effect is not always good. Sometimes it's chaos!

Having the new skateboard inspires you to try some new tricks ...

**Rainforests** are an important part of our world. What happens in them and the effects are important for all of us.

The rainforest is a massive tangle of causes and effects. For example:

Rain falls in the forest.

= tropical rainforests

= temperate rainforests

The water allows plants to grow and animals to drink.

## Sometimes, though, the effect of an action is chaos:

People cut down the trees on a steep slope.

With no tree roots to keep the soil in place, a landslide happens.

# Soaked!

You would expect a rainforest to be rainy – that's how it got its name, after all. But rainforests are not just wet. They are part of a system called a water cycle.

The cycle begins in the morning, when the Sun comes up.

As it gets higher the air cools, and the water it contains forms clouds.

The Sun heats the air and the forest becomes hot.

## The forest's warm, wet air rises.

As the next day heats up, the warm, wet air rises to form clouds again.

If the temperature rises too much, though, less rain falls. If this happens often, parts of the rainforest dry out and disappear.

## Disaster!

Eventually the water-filled clouds drop their load in a deluge of rain.

(It's a good idea to be under cover when this happens.)

The rain drips down to the rainforest floor and into the soil.

Water in the soil is absorbed by the rainforest trees and plants.

7

# Raging Rivers

As well as from clouds formed close by, rainforests get water from clouds that have formed over the sea.

The Amazon rainforest, for example, gets extra water from clouds born over the Atlantic Ocean. And all that extra water has to go somewhere ...

When rain drips onto the forest floor some creeps downhill, creating small streams.

The streams feed rainforest rivers.

The biggest rainforest river, the Amazon, could fill about 2,000 swimming pools per second.

Small rivers feed into **bigger ones,** which flow towards the sea. A huge amount of water flows

*downstream.*

The power of flowing water can be used to make electricity, so hydro-electric dams are sometimes built on rainforest rivers.

When water from the dam is released it flows to the sea. The process begins again.

The dams flood large areas of forest. The plants, animals and people that live there lose their home.

# The Fight for Light

One crucial ingredient for a rainforest is rain. The other is (of course) trees.

In a tropical rainforest, the trees have to grow quickly. They need to escape the gloomy forest floor and reach life-giving sunshine as soon as possible.

When it reaches the canopy, the tree spreads out its branches and leaves to catch the light.

## Canopy

The seedling grows quickly through the dense plants of the understorey and towards the light.

## Understorey

Trees start life as tiny seedlings on the forest floor.

Right away they are in danger: seedlings are a tasty snack for rainforest animals.

Buttress roots

Some trees keep on growing, into the clear air above the canopy.

Water is harder to get above the canopy, so in dry times the tallest trees shed their leaves to prevent water loss.

If the weather gets too dry, forest fires start.

Millions of rainforest trees a year are destroyed by fire, causing *chaos* for the animals who live there.

# Look out Below!

When a new clearing appears in the rainforest, the brazil-nut tree has a clever process for making sure it fills the space.

The only trouble is, it can be a bit hazardous if you happen to be walking past at a crucial moment ...

The brazil-nut tree produces seed pods. The pods are a long way up from the ground.

When the pods are ripe they drop to the ground. They weigh the same as a small cannonball.

60 metres tall

Brazil nut

Look out below!

To survive the landing the pods have to be really strong. Only the agouti has teeth that can chew through to the seeds inside.

**Agouti**

The agouti eats some seeds and hides others for later. But sometimes agoutis forget where they put their seeds.

The seeds stay hidden for years, until a clearing appears above and sunlight reaches the forest floor.

The sunlight signals the seeds to start growing.

The seedlings have to grow fast. If the *sunlight* is blocked by other plants, they may not survive.

# Piranha Danger!

Tropical rainforests are hot and sweaty. But anyone tempted to go for a swim to cool down should think twice! Predators lurk in the cloudy water.

Among the most famous is a fearsome little fish: the Amazonian piranha. But how does the piranha hunt?

If something plops into the water nearby, the piranhas sense it and investigate.

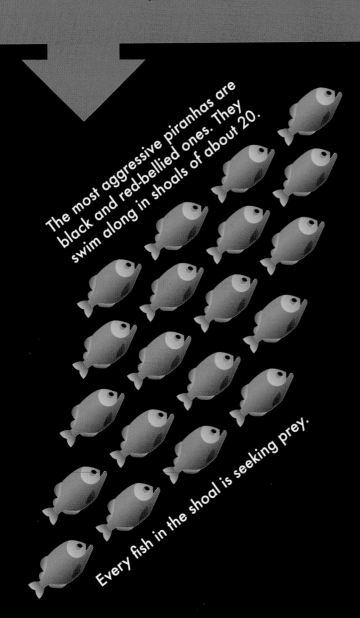

The most aggressive piranhas are black and red-bellied ones. They swim along in shoals of about 20.

Every fish in the shoal is seeking prey.

Scientists have discovered that red-bellied piranhas bark and gnash their teeth to threaten other fish.

# If there is **blood** in the water, the piranhas smell it.

Piranhas can smell one drop of blood in a bathtub full of water, so a bleeding animal is like a sign for lunch.

The shoal attacks. Their sharp teeth bite into their prey.

The piranhas concentrate on the attack. They should watch out, though!

Piranhas' teeth often fall out or break. When this happens, new ones replace them.

**Piranha** is one of the spectacled caiman's favourite meals. A caiman could sneak up on them at any minute.

# Ant Antics

In the rainforest, ants are everywhere. There are edible ants that taste like lemons, bullet ants whose bite is like being shot, and ferocious army ants that devour anything in their path.

There are also, of course, ordinary ants. Every ant in their colony has a job that's aimed at making sure the colony continues.

Ant nest

When a scout *senses food*, it follows the smell to its source. Ants love sweet plant nectar.

The colony's main need is food. Specialist scout ants set off across the forest floor, sniffing for anything edible.

Ants smell using their antennae.

When the scout finds nectar, it heads back to the colony. It lays a scent trail using chemicals called pheromones.

Pheromones

A column of worker ants sets out to collect the nectar. More and more ants follow the scent trail and climb into the plant. But it's **a trap!**

Since the scout visited, it has rained. The sides of the plant are slippery, so the ants cannot climb back out.

And this is a pitcher plant – **it's carnivorous!** The fluid in the bottom slowly melts the ants into ant soup, which the plant digests.

Help!

# Tiger Alert!

Some of the world's biggest cats live in rainforests. The forests of South Asia are home to the biggest of all – the tiger.

Tigers are **apex predators**. They are at the top of the food chain. At the bottom of the chain are much smaller animals.

Lion-tailed macaque

The plants are eaten by monkeys such as the lion-tailed macaque and deer such as the Indian muntjac.

Indian muntjac

The chain begins with plants, which grow quickly in the warm, wet forest.

Young deer are sometimes attacked and killed by Indian wild boar. Boar will eat almost anything, from fruit and nuts to snakes and lizards.

If they are eating young deer, the boars need to watch out for tigers. Tigers eat deer, as well as monkeys, birds, fish ... and boar.

# Nothing preys on tigers

– except humans. Every year, people kill hundreds of tigers.

So many have died that there is a risk tigers may become extinct.

# Slash and Burn

Many people who live in rainforests grow their own food. To clear land for planting crops they use a system called slash and burn.

The slash-and-burn process usually starts during the driest part of the year.

First people chop down most of the plants and trees. They leave any that could provide food or timber.

As the driest part of the year ends, it is set aflame.

The chopped-down vegetation is left to dry in the sun.

20

## As soon as the ashes have cooled,

crops are planted. Rainforest soil does not contain many nutrients, and the ashes provide some extra ones.

The crops get plenty of water when the wet season starts. This and the extra nutrients mean they grow quickly.

As they grow, the crops use up the nutrients in the soil. After a year or two, these nutrients have gone and crops will not grow.

## The people have to clear a new piece of land.

If too much land is cleared, the soil never recovers. Trees cannot grow and part of the rainforest **disappears forever.**

# First Contact

A hundred years ago, few people from outside came to rainforests. Today though, settlers, loggers, miners and others are moving in.

When outsiders arrive, they make 'first contact' with undiscovered tribes – often with catastrophic results.

For example, newcomers arrived when a road was built into the territory of the Paraná people in Brazil.

*cough, cough*

The Paraná came out of the forest to meet the strangers. Some of the newcomers had brought with them diseases such as colds, flu and measles.

New road

Cough, cough

The Paraná caught the new diseases. They had not experienced them before and had no immunity.

Roughly half the Paraná quickly died. The government airlifted the survivors to new lands, away from the road.

The deaths continued in the new lands.
In the end, 80 per cent of the tribe died.

Twenty years after they had been forced to leave, the remaining Paraná returned to their homeland.

# Orangutan Orphans

Rainforest soil is not ideal for growing crops, but one that does grow well is oil palm.

The oil is used in thousands of products: foods, soaps and cosmetics. But oil palm plantations cause problems for the rainforest plants and animals – including orangutans.

*oil palm*

During the land clearance, big animals such as tigers, elephants and orangutans, are killed to get them out of the way.

If the animals have young, these are killed or sold as pets. Baby orangutans can be *sold for hundreds of dollars.*

Before planting oil palms, the farmers clear the rainforest of other trees and plants.

In Indonesia and Malaysia, clearing land for oil palm plantations is now the biggest cause of *forest destruction.*

Some orangutans
are rescued from the
pet trade and taken to
*animal centres.*

At the centres they grow up in safety,
learning to *live in the wild.*

When they are ready to look after
themselves, the orangutans are
released back into the rainforest.

# Forest gold

The riverbanks and beaches of the Amazon contain gold. It washed downriver from the Andes mountains centuries ago.

Today, thousands of gold prospectors are at work in the Amazon. They are causing big problems in the rainforest.

Mercury, a liquid metal, is added to the barrels. It picks up any remaining bits of gold, which are then removed.

Large bits of gold are picked out, then the leftover water is put in barrels.

gold

The miners start by setting up a water cannon. The water cannon blasts off soil, which is channelled away.

Hose

The water, which still contains mercury, is tipped into nearby rivers.

Small fish absorb some of the mercury.

Big fish, birds and caimans eat a lot of smaller fish, so they collect a lot of mercury.

Caiman

People living nearby catch and eat the fish – as well as the mercury they contain.

**Mercury damages** the central nervous system of living creatures. It also causes harm to their unborn young.

# Tim-ber!

The world's rainforests are shrinking. Their trees are cut down to sell the timber, or to clear land for farming.

Cutting down rainforest causes damage to the environment everywhere on Earth.

The carbon they contain is released into the atmosphere as carbon dioxide.

$CO_2$

$O_2$

Some trees and plants are burned, to clear the ground.

The biggest trees have the most carbon stored in their structures. When they are cut down, they can no longer take in carbon dioxide.

As trees grow, they take in carbon dioxide ($CO_2$) from the air and release oxygen ($O_2$). They store the carbon in their structure.

28

The carbon dioxide rises into the atmosphere, where it joins a layer of greenhouse gases. This layer stops heat escaping into space.

The trapped heat is slowly causing Earth's temperature to rise. This is called global warming.

Ice cap

Sea-level rises

**Global warming** is causing deserts to spread, an increase in violent storms and hurricanes, melting ice caps, and sea-level rises, leading to floods and loss of land.

Hurricanes

# glossary

**airlifted** taken somewhere in a helicopter or aeroplane

**apex predator** animal at the top of the food chain. It is not hunted by other animals in its natural environment

**canopy** the top layer of leaves and branches in a forest

**central nervous system** network of nerves that controls a body's movement. In animals with a backbone, the core of the central nervous system is the brain and spinal column

**colony** group of living things that has moved to an area to live there

**cosmetics** beauty products used to improve a person's appearance or create an image

**deluge** sudden fall of a lot of rain

**extinct** no longer in existence; completely died out

**global warming** increase in the average temperature of Earth's atmosphere

**greenhouse gas** gas that traps warmth in Earth's atmosphere

**hydro-electric** using the movement of water to make electricity

**ice cap** frozen areas at the North and South poles

**immunity** ability to resist a disease

**nutrient** something used by living things to stay alive and for growth

**orphan** a person or an animal whose parents died while they were a baby or child

**prospector** person looking for precious minerals, such as gold

**plantation** area planted with all the same kind of trees or other crop

**shoal** group of fish

**understorey** the plants growing above the forest floor but below the canopy

**water cannon** large, powerful hose that produces a forceful jet of water

# Finding out more

## Rainforest places

**The Eden Project**
Bodelva
St Austell
Cornwall PL24 2SG

At the Eden Project you will find the largest indoor rainforest in the world. Filled with tropical heat, the Rainforest Biome is 15,000 m² of rainforest trees and plants, which you can see from ground level or the elevated walkway. Website at: **www.edenproject.com**

**The Living Rainforest**
Hampstead Norreys
Thatcham
Berkshire RG18 0TN

Spread across three large glasshouses, The Living Forest contains hundreds of different rainforest plants and animals. From fish to monkeys, Chinese water dragons to Harry the armadillo, there is always plenty to see. The website is at: **https://livingrainforest.org/**

## Rainforest books

*100 Facts Rainforests*, Camilla de la Bedoyere (Miles Kelly, 2016)
Crammed with amazing facts, detailed artwork, things to make and do, and cartoons that add a bit of fun.

*Rainforest Rough Guide*, Paul Mason (Bloomsbury, 2011)
A series of emails from an explorer deep in the Amazon rainforest gives details about how she is surviving and some of her amazing discoveries. A great, fun read that makes it easy to imagine what it must be like hunting for jaguars, poisonous creatures and other rainforest rarities.

*Where on Earth? Rainforests*, Susie Brooks (Wayland, 2016)
This book takes you on a journey through the world's rainforests, from Costa Rica to the Amazon, Africa to Australia. On the way you'll find out about the plants and animals that make the rainforest special, different types of rainforest, and all kinds of other information about these amazing places.

# Index